BASTIEN PIANO BAS[ICS]

PERFORMANCE
LEVEL 4

BY JANE SMISOR BASTIEN

Contents

*To reinforce the feeling of achievement, the teacher or student may put a √ when the page has been mastered.

ISBN 0-8497-5279-5

© **1985 Kjos West**, 4382 Jutland Drive, San Diego, California 92117. International copyright secured. All rights reserved. Printed in U.S.A.

WARNING! All the music, text, art, and graphics in this book are protected by copyright law. To copy or reproduce them by any method is an infringement of the copyright law. Anyone who reproduces copyrighted matter is subject to substantial penalties and assessments for each infringement.

R & R Music Centre Ltd.

Pink Clouds

Throwing Snowballs

Coronation March

Misty Moon

T.I.* Boogie

Steady boogie beat

Use with page 18 of Piano, Level 4.

*Triad Inversion

Up-Hill Race

Allegro con spirito

Classic Encounter

Use with pages 20-21 of Piano, *Level 4.*

The Palace Gardens

Minuet

from *Don Giovanni*

Wolfgang Amadeus Mozart

Easy Livin'

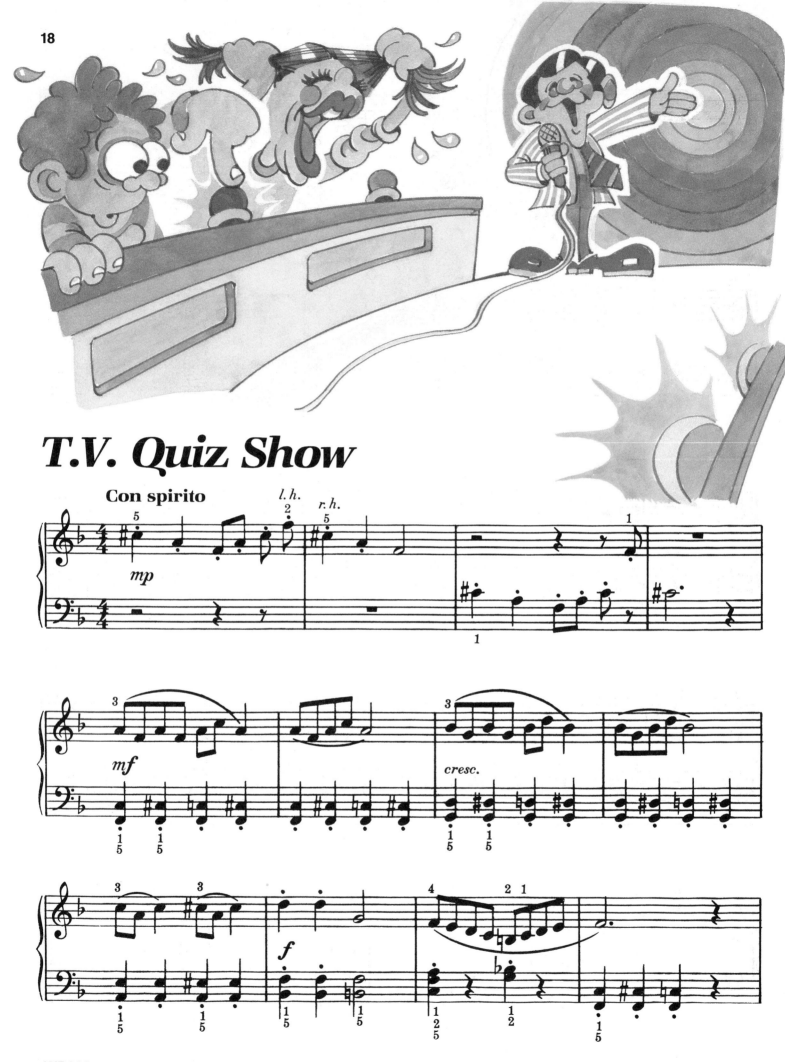

T.V. Quiz Show

Turkey in the Straw

Con spirito

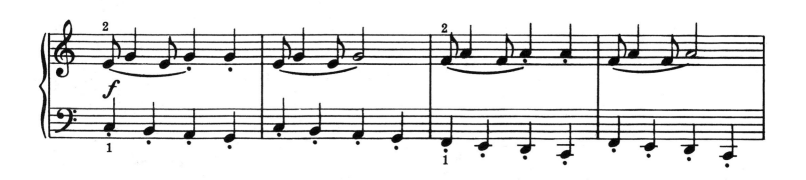

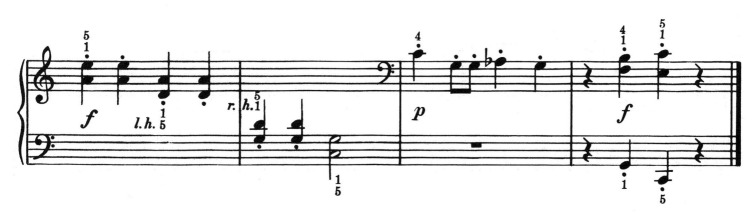

Hernando's Hideaway

Allegro con spirito

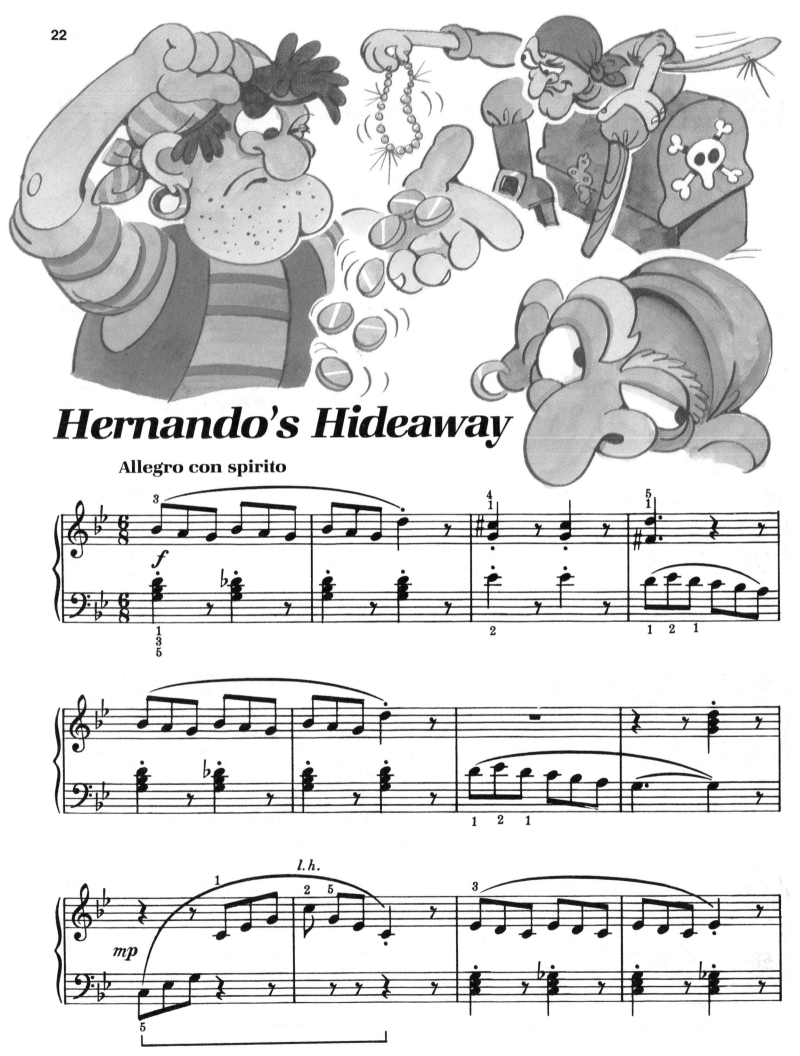

Stately Giraffes

The Roaming Cowboy

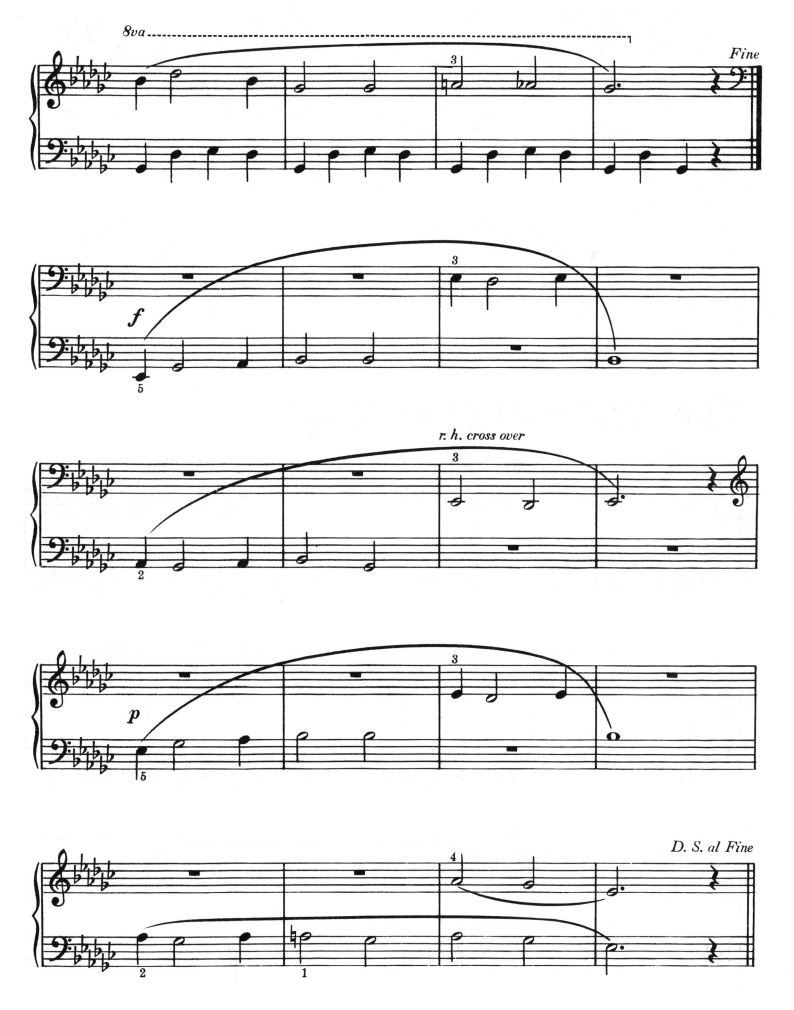

Battle Hymn of the Republic

Water Lilies

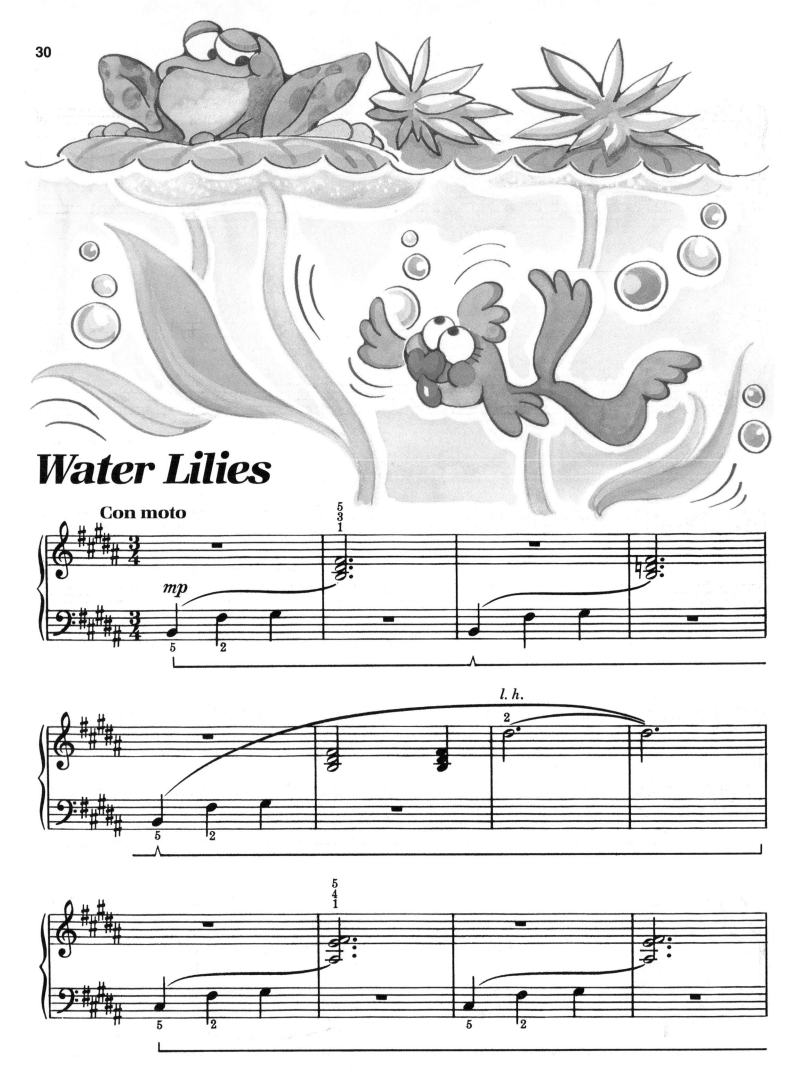

When the Saints Go Marching In

Con spirito